How do I use this scheme?

Key Words with Peter and Jane has three
parallel series, each containing twelve books. All three
series are written using the same carefully controlled
vocabulary. Readers will get the most out of **Key Words** with
Peter and Jane when they follow the books in the pattern
1a, 1b, 1c; 2a, 2b, 2c and so on.

• Series a
gradually introduces and repeats new words.

• Series b
provides further practice of these same words, but
in a different context and with different illustrations.

• Series c
uses familiar words to teach **phonics** in a methodical way,
enabling children to read increasingly difficult words.
It also provides a link to writing.

LADYBIRD BOOKS

UK | USA | Canada | Ireland | Australia
India | New Zealand | South Africa

Ladybird Books is part of the Penguin Random House group of companies
whose addresses can be found at global.penguinrandomhouse.com.

www.penguin.co.uk   www.puffin.co.uk   www.ladybird.co.uk

First published 1964
This edition 2009, 2014, 2016
Copyright © Ladybird Books Ltd, 1964
001

A CIP catalogue record for this book is
available from the British Library

ISBN: 978-1-409-30128-8

Printed in China

Key Words

with Peter and Jane

7c

Easy to sound

written by W. Murray
illustrated by J.H. Wingfield

ee

We know the word: **see.**

There are two sounds in the word **see.**
They are **s** and **ee.**

s-ee make **see.**

We can make the sounds **b** and **ee.**

b-ee make **bee.**

Now we can read:

1   Here is a bee.

2   The boy sees the bee.

3   He lets the bee go free.

4   He sees the bee go by the tree.

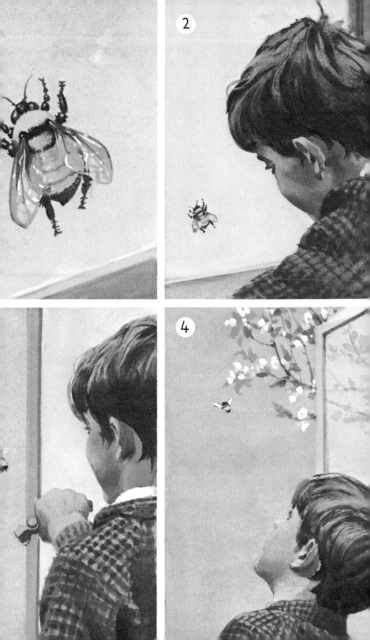

OO

We know the word: **look**.

The sounds **l**, **oo**, **k** are in the word **look**.

l-oo-k make **look**,

b-oo-k make **book**,

c-oo-k make **cook**.

Now we can read:

1   Here is a book.

2   The girl wants to cook.

3   She looks in the book.

4   What she sees in the book helps her to cook.

We know the words: **bring, king** and **going.**

They all end in the sound **ing.**

Now we can read:

1   The king has a ring.

2   The man is fishing.

3   The boy is jumping.

4   The woman is reading.

We know the words: **shop**, **she**, **fish** and **wish**.

They all have the sound **sh**.

Now we can read:

1   She looks in the shop.

2   This shop is shut.

3   She has some shells.

4   The fish is in the dish.

Complete the words as you write
them in your exercise book. The
pictures will help you.

ee oo ing sh

1 r - - k

2 w - - -

3 bru - -

4 tr - -

5 r - - -

6 h - - k

7 thr - -

8 di - -

The answers are on Page 48.

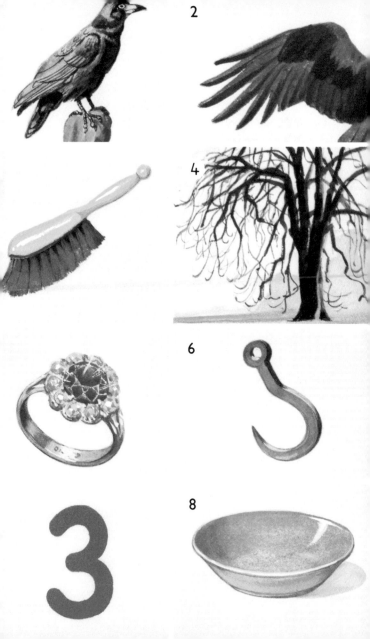

2

4

6

8

3

ea

1   We know the word: **tea.**
    The sounds **t-ea** make the word
    tea.

2   Put the sound **t** after the sound **ea**
    and you make the word **eat.**

3   We know the word: **sea.**
    The sounds **s-ea** make **sea.**

4   The sounds **s-ea-t** make the word
    seat.

5   The sounds **m-ea-t** make the word
    meat.

6   The sounds **t-ea-p-o-t** make the
    word **teapot.**

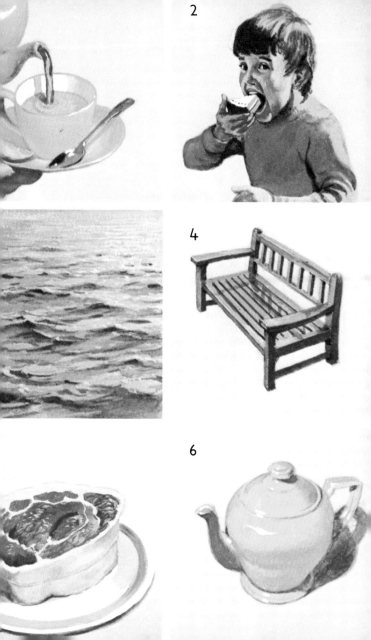

2

4

6

1   We know the word: **chair**.
    When we start to say **chair** we
    make the sound **ch**.

2   We know the word: **children**.
    We make the sound **ch** when we
    start to say **children**.

3   We know the sounds **ea** and **ch**.
    ea-ch make the word **each**.
    Each boy has an apple.

4   The sounds **r-ea-ch** make the word
    reach.

5   The sounds **p-ea-ch** make the word
    peach.

6   The children each reach for a
    peach.

er

We know the words: **Peter, flower, her, brother, sister, mother, father, water.**

They all end in the sound **er.**

1 We can make all the sounds **t, ea, ch, er.**

The sounds **t-ea-ch-er** make **teacher.**

2 We know the words fish and man. Now we can make **fish-er-man.** The fisherman is on the pier.

We know the words: farm, help, play and round. Now we can read:

3 Here is a farmer.

4 The farmer has a helper.

5 Here is a player.

6 The children play rounders.

2

4

6

We know the words: **all, ball, call, tell, well, will, hill, doll, pull.**
They all end in the sound **ll**.

Now we can read:

1 The men are by the wall.
   They are all tall.

2 The farmer pulls the bull.

3 The bull pulls the farmer.

4 The teacher gives the boy the bell.

5 The boy rings the bell.

6 He draws a hill and a road.
   Then he draws a mill on the hill.

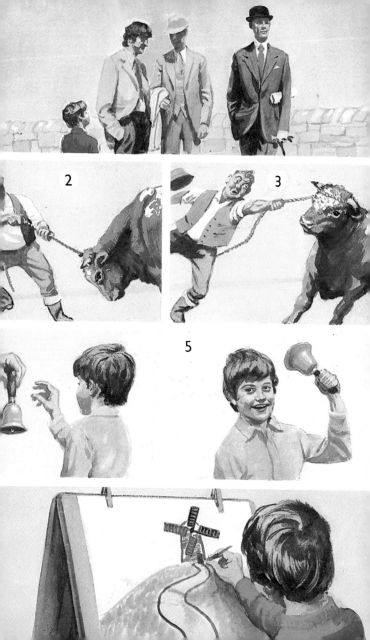

Complete the words as you write
them in your exercise book. The
pictures will help you.

ea   ch   er   ll

1 b - - ch   2 pat - -

3 we - -   4 l - - f

5 keep - -   6 be - -

7 mat - -   8 numb -

The answers are on Page 48.

2

4

6

8

Jane draws a man and two children in a fish and chip shop.

"Look, Peter," she says. "The children are in a fish and chip shop. The man asks the children if they want fish with their chips."

Peter writes the letters **bed**.

"This word is bed," he says. Then he makes the word look like the picture of a bed.

"Our teacher did this at school," he says. "It helps us to write **b** and **d**."

Then Peter draws a man on the bed.

-e

Peter has the letter **e** on a card.

He says, "I can make **fir** into **fire** with the **e** on this card."

Then he puts the **e** at the end of another word.

"Look," he says, "the **e** at the end makes **pip** into **pipe**. It can make

can into **cane**

pan into **pane**

van into **vane**

fir into **fire**

tub into **tube**

and

pin into **pine**."

We know the words: **thank**, **think** **three**.

They all start with the sound **th**.

Now we can read:

1 The blue book is thin.

2 This is a thick book.

3 Here is a moth.

4 He has good teeth.

5 It is thick cloth.

6 The number is thirty.

7 The man makes a path.

8 The boy has a bath.

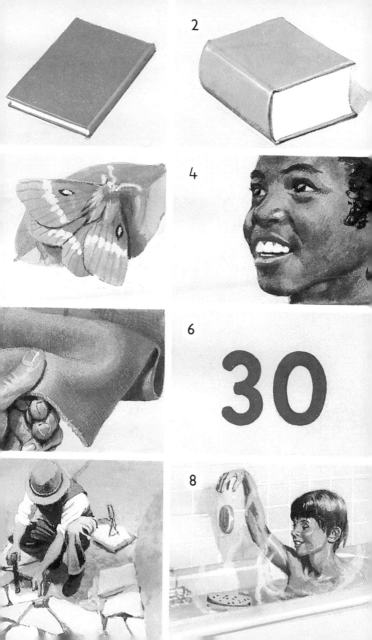

2

4

6

30

8

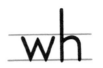

wh

We know the words: **what**, **where**, **which**, **when**, **why**.

They all start with the sound **wh**.

Now we can read:

1 He has a whip for his top.

2 The farmer looks at his wheat.

3 Here is a whale in the sea.

4 He puts the wheel on the car.

5 This is a whisk.

6 The cat has whiskers.

7 The boy has a whistle.

8 The girl whispers to her friend.

Peter and Jane have just had some pictures from their aunt and uncle of their holiday by the sea. There is a letter from Aunty with the pictures. They read the letter in which Aunty tells them that she and Uncle are well. She sends her love to Peter and Jane and their mother and father. Aunty tells them that they may keep the pictures as a present from her. She thinks that the pictures are very good.

"We must write and thank her," says Jane.

"Yes, all right," says Peter, "but let us look at the pictures first and then we will write to Aunty and Uncle."

Copy out and complete —

1 The --ildren have some pictures to l--k at.

2 --e has sent them a lett--.

3 Aunty te--s them to k--p the pictures.

4 They are read--- the letter.

5 They will writ- to --ank Aunty.

The answers are on Page 48.

The first picture is of the children on the sands, as they go along in a donkey cart. It is an old green cart with big red wheels. Peter and Jane had never been in this donkey cart before.

In the picture the donkey has a hat. On his back he has a red cloth with bells on it. The bells ring as the donkey pulls the cart along. There is a whip in the cart.

"It was a dear little donkey," says Jane. "I do like donkeys."

"It did not go very fast," says Peter, "but it was fun."

Copy out and complete—

1   The donkey pu--s the cart.
2   The wh--ls are red and the cart is gr--n.
3   The bells r--- as the cart is go--- along.
4   A clo-- is on the donkey's back.
5   There is a --ip in the cart.

The answers are on Page 49.

Here are some fishing boats going out. The sun is going down as the motor boats put out to sea. Some birds are flying over the fishing boats. The fishermen hope to bring back many fish for the shops. Then there will be fish for anyone to buy and the fishermen will have money.

In the picture, Peter and Jane sit on a wall by the beach with their uncle as they look at the boats. Peter has his kite in his hand.

As he looks at the picture, Peter says he would like to go out with the fishing boats one day.

Copy out and complete—

1 They l--k at the fish--- boats.

2 Peter and Jane are by the b--ch.

3 Peter has his kit- in his hand.

4 The fish--men hop- to bring back many fish.

5 There will be fi-- for anyone to buy.

The answers are on Page 49.

This is a picture of the fishermen. Peter and Jane are not in it. The fishermen have come back with many fish in their boats. It is the morning after Peter and Jane saw the fishing boats go out to sea.

The fishermen are working to get the fish out of the boats. They want to get the fish into the shops as soon as they can.

"Would you like to work like that?" Jane asks Peter.

"Yes, why not?" says Peter. "I think the men get good pay for their work. They can have a bath and put on other clothes after it."

Copy out and complete—

1   The boats have been out to s - -
2   It is the morn - - - after they saw the boats go out.
3   They want to get the fish into the - - ops.
4   He thinks the men get g - - d money for their work.
5   They can have a ba - - after their work.

The answers are on Page 49.

This is an old mill which Peter and Jane saw when on holiday with their aunt and uncle. A big water wheel works the mill. Aunty and Uncle like to go to the woods, or to this place for a picnic tea when it is very hot.

"We had never been there before," said Jane. "It was nice by the trees. It was not too hot there, but I should not like to go into the water. There would be danger from the mill wheel."

"There were many fish in the water," said Peter. "That man who was fishing had five by the end of the afternoon."

Copy out and complete—

1   It is a picture of an old mi--.

2   Peter and Jane like a picnic t--.

3   They had nev-- been there before.

4   In the picture there is a man fish---.

5   It is the wheel whi-- works the mill.

The answers are on Page 50.

The children always like playing on the beach. It is best when the sun is out and it is hot. Then the children can take off their clothes to go into the sea or to run and play on the sands.

In the picture you can see some donkeys, Punch and Judy, an ice-cream van and the pier. Some children are out in a boat with Jack, and others are looking for shells.

Peter has a jumping game with some other boys. Jane and her friend play with a new, red ball. They all look very happy.

Copy out and complete—

1   They like play --- on the b --ch.

2   It is hot --en the sun is out.

3   Some --ildren look for --ells.

4   You can s-- some donkeys.

5   Peter and Jane will put their pictures in a b--k.

The answers are on Page 50.

When they have seen all the pictures, the children each write to their aunt and uncle to thank them for their letter and the pictures. They tell them how happy they were to be on holiday with them.

Peter writes to his uncle that they are all fit and well and that he and Jane have been to the Zoo. Jane tells Aunty about some new clothes she has had.

Then she writes, "Mum and I are going to make some jam. She lets me help her to cook. Dad thinks he would like to keep bees and he has found a book to read about bees. His friend keeps bees."

Copy out and complete—

1 They --ch write a letter.

2 Jane helps h-- mother to c--k.

3 They are all fit and w---.

4 Dad --inks he would like to keep b--s.

5 He reads a book --ich will help him.

The answers are on Page 50.

It is four o'clock. The sun is out again. There has been no rain for days. The two children go out to send off their letters. On their way back they call on a friend. He is going to make a go-cart with some wheels he has found. He tells Peter and Jane that his father will help him to make the go-cart.

"I saw one in a shop," says Peter.

"Yes," says his friend, "in some shops they call them Go-Karts. Some Go-Karts have motors in them and others do not."

Copy out and complete—

1   It is not rain - - -.

2   They send off their lett - - s.

3   He has found some - -eels.

4   His father wi - - help him.

5   He saw a Go-Kart in a - -op.

The answers are on Page 51.

Pages 48 to 51 give the answers to the written exercises in this book.

Page 12

1	rook	2	wing
3	brush	4	tree
5	ring	6	hook
7	three	8	dish

Page 22

1	beach	2	patch
3	well	4	leaf
5	keeper	6	bell
7	match	8	number

Page 32

1 The children have some pictures to look at.

2 She has sent them a letter.

3 Aunty tells them to keep the pictures.

4 They are reading the letter.

5 They will write to thank Aunty.

Page 34

1 The donkey pulls the cart.

2 The wheels are red and the cart is green.

3 The bells ring as the cart is going along.

4 A cloth is on the donkey's back.

5 There is a whip in the cart.

Page 36

1 They look at the fishing boats.

2 Peter and Jane are by the beach.

3 Peter has his kite in his hand.

4 The fishermen hope to bring back many fish.

5 There will be fish for anyone to buy.

Page 38

1 The boats have been out to sea.

2 It is the morning after they saw the boats go out.

3 They want to get the fish into the shops.

4 He thinks the men get good money for their work.

5 They can have a bath after their work.

Page 40

1   It is a picture of an old mill.

2   Peter and Jane like a picnic tea.

3   They had never been there before.

4   In the picture there is a man fishing.

5   It is the wheel which works the mill.

Page 42

1   They like playing on the beach.

2   It is hot when the sun is out.

3   Some children look for shells.

4   You can see some donkeys.

5   Peter and Jane will put their pictures in a book.

Page 44

1   They each write a letter.

2   Jane helps her mother to cook.

3   They are all fit and well.

4   Dad thinks he would like to keep bees.

5   He reads a book which will help him.

Page 46

1 It is not raining.

2 They send off their letters.

3 He has found some wheels.

4 His father will help him.

5 He saw a Go-Kart in a shop.

Revision of sounds
learned in this book

ee oo

ing sh

ea ch er ll

-e th wh

Now read Book 8a

Learning by sounds

If children learn the sounds of letters and how to blend them with the other letter sounds (eg. c-a-t) they can tackle new words independently (eg. P-a-t).

In the initial stages it is best if these phonic words are already known to the learner.

However, not all English words can be learned in this way as the English language is not purely phonetic (eg. t-h-e).

In general a 'mixed' approach to reading is recommended. Some words are learned by blending the sounds of their letters and others by look-and-say, whole word or sentence methods.

This book provides the link with writing for the words in Readers 7a and 7b.